When the Wildflowers Wilted

Hannah Farmer

BookLeaf Publishing

India | USA | UK

Presentation by *BookLeaf Publishing*

Web: www.bookleafpub.com

E-mail: info@bookleafpub.com

ISBN: 9789358735185

First edition 2023

*To mom, who encouraged me to keep a pen
in my hand.*

Breaking Up

I find it kind of funny how every time we fight
You always wanna be right.
Sometimes it's overwhelming, controlling,
asserting might
If you would just talk with me, we could find the
light.

I don't know what I saw in you at the start,
I did say I was a bit tart.
But still, you stole my heart
I made it look like art.

Now I'm left in the dust once again
I'm off to start again.
Abandoned by my closest friend,
You always knew it had to end.

Perfect

Dark Museum Corridors.
Unacceptable whispers
On me and you,
Perfect in every way.

Midnight Regret

Should I text her? I really can't tell,
My fingers hover nervously
Over the blinking keyboard
Where nothing is written.
This is all her fault.
But she also
Thinks the same
About
Me.

[untitled]

4

I am a bad, bad person.
I am not even a person, I'm just a woman.

The Girl

The girl who bought a ticket to see
Her favorite artist was really
The girl who picked up a magazine when she
was 9
And saw an album cover that she thought was
cool.

The girl who bought a movie
Ticket wasn't allowed to play with
Dolls.

The girl who got married young was really the
girl
Who pretended to be the mayor,
Surgeon, police chief, and
Journalist in her pretend town.

The girl today who is taking
A nap in the afternoon is
Really the girl who created
Extra homework assignments for
Herself because she got bored.

The girl who wanted to fall
Asleep while reading with her

Mom is really the girl who just
Needed independence and decided
It was the only thing that
Could set her apart

Toxic Relationship

"I find it kind of funny"
"I think it's funny too"
"How every time we seem to fight"
"I pass the blame to you?"

"Yes, you've got the idea."
"I'm sorry, I think you're wrong."
"The only thing I'm wrong about"
"Was me staying with you this long."

"No, no, this isn't right,"
"Was this not what you wanted?"
"Why are you getting mad?"
"I thought that's what you intended."

"Why do you want to leave me now?"
"I think you know the answer."
"Am I too volatile for you to love?"
"You control me like a cancer."

Winter

The hours turn into the cold.
Mist echoes through the day,
Our green earth begins to fold.

The sun's not out to hold,
The leaves have gone away.
The hours turn into the cold.

The wind is sterner than a scold.
Tree hands clasped to pray,
Our green earth begins to fold.

The bit of ice is uncontrolled,
Grass begs the sun to stay.
The hours turn into the cold.

Flowers set in a frozen mold,
Nature made harder than clay,
Our green earth begins to fold.

The sun retreats to her abode,
The ice begins her decay.
The hours turn into the cold,
Our green earth begins to fold.

Hot Chocolate Days

Summer is when love
Is supposed to start
Beating heart
And sometimes it does.

But I think winter
Could be something better
Like beginning a forever
Or a kiss in the snow.

Nights by a campfire
Could be romantic
Or naps in a hammock
Abstract glances.

But hot chocolate days
Snowmen and frozen fingers
Frozen hugs, and glances that linger
And love spun in it all.

Nobody Knows

Nobody knows what would have happened
If we had stayed.
If please fell on deaf ears.
Compromise stabbed and sacrificed on the altar
of unity.
So shiny on the outside, falling to pieces
everywhere else.

The unforgiving gravel under the van scolding
you with each crunch.
A clandestine secret held over my head
Like an egg over a pan.
A pan that is hot and full of grease,
But that needs the egg to drop before it spits out
at you.

Why am I giving you a poem? You don't deserve
it.
I'm glad we left.
I'll go on to do great things. But you?
What good are you going to achieve?
What benefits?
What will you offer to this miserable life?
Nobody knows.

Jellyfish

If your hand was in my hair,
Then I would forget
The windshield that cracked in the hailstorm
And the way my cat jumped
And knocked over my trash can.

I would be floating in the ocean,
The jellyfish creating choreography to mimic
The way our bodies move
With each other.

Your hand may mess up my hair,
But the water was going to do that anyway.

Look! A jellyfish is swimming by us!

Flowers and Monsters

12

In my dreams,
I am running away from a monster
With the head shaped like a flower
But it wilts away each hour.

And one day the flower will burst,
Showering the ground.
I'll look around
In awe and panic.

While the pieces settle
And the grass gives way with a moan
I'll try to collect them all
But I can't collect them all.

I need them, I need them!
I can't create a life
Without my dreams.
Even if they're filled with
Flowers and monsters
And nothing is what it seems.

The Night Before I Moved Away

The night before I moved away
I saw a movie with my mom.
I drove home in her car,
Feeling like an 11 year old on
The way home from volleyball.

I sat on the swing set,
Watching stars take over the sky
And said hello to three-year old me
Who was just learning to swing.

Then she hopped off the swing
And ran into the night.
And I'm not sure if I'll ever
Get to meet her again.

Boxes

One week is 7 days.

5 days of class. Church. Cleaning.
2 days for the weekend.

Sometime, a long time ago, I
Tried to relegate you into a
Weekly box.
Homework, test, clean.
You.
But you don't fit a weekly box.
You make up the other boxes.

So now I'll check off the other
Boxes and run home to you.
You smell like your room and
I can't wait to hug you.

Just one more week.
Just a few boxes.

Send This Back to the Kitchen

Here I am, in this same familiar place.
The hallway guides me to the same
Lights that I walked past before,
And even the room is the exact same.

I haven't slept more than two
Hours in the last two days,
And I drove the whole way,
Again. And when I hear screaming,
It isn't even unsettling.

I didn't even cry
For hours and hours and almost
Two whole days.
But the same babble spun a web
Through the whole place
And that was my last straw.
I can't even explain why.

Now a ghost lives in my house
And is not seen or heard.
It is all quite proper.
It is all quite unfamiliar.

I think I'll take what we had before.
Send this back to the kitchen,
It's not made right.

Stargazing in the Suburbs

Stars and rainbows and smiles
Hanging in the bright night sky.
Everyone says young love is special,
A gift not quite unwrapped.

Sometimes it takes a lot of work
To peel through the layers,
Scratch off the tape,
To find the gift on the inside.

Like going stargazing in the suburbs.
You have to look for stars carefully
And sometimes you're tricked by airplanes
But the real stars are so beautiful.

Or reading an old book
Looking up unknown words
Plodding through descriptions
For the glorious conclusion.

And it's so worth it
Because you are my gift
My perfect star
My glorious forever ending.

Second Priority

I can take second priority for everyone else,
But I'm not first even for myself.
I'll give all the positive to everyone I see,
So only the negative is left for me.
Selfless, loving, caring, kind,
All qualities so hard to find.
And I'm not that naïve
That I think these words all describe me.
But I'll stay up all night to make people okay,
Then spend the day in a painful haze.
But where can I find the delicate balance
Between sacrificial love, and personal valiance?
I guess I'll just try to love and care,
Even if I don't have enough happiness to share.
I know I'll never deserve any better,
So I'll try to stay helpful forever.

I'll Remember You

When the sun meets the sky
And the ocean meets the moon
And the stars start coming out
Then I'll remember you

Even though you're so far away
Never to be seen again
When the stars start shining
I'll remember you then.

Oxymoronic Acrostic

Calm hands, steady heartbeat.
Already at rest.
Fireflies dancing,
Fireflies lighting up the night.
Ethereal threads of silver moonlight,
Incandescent stars.
Nothing moves,
All is calm.
Time freezes, trapped in a loop.
Evening ends, night begins.
Dancing stars, finally laid to rest.

www.ingramcontent.com/pod-product-compliance
Lightning Source LLC
LaVergne TN
LVHW051252200726
843510LV00011B/1816